That Was Now,
This Is Then

Also by Vijay Seshadri

Wild Kingdom
The Long Meadow
The Disappearances
3 Sections

That Was Now,
This Is Then

poems

Vijay Seshadri

Graywolf Press

This publication is made possible, in part, by the voters of Minnesota through a Minnesota State Arts Board Operating Support grant, thanks to a legislative appropriation from the arts and cultural heritage fund. Significant support has also been provided by Target Foundation, the McKnight Foundation, the Lannan Foundation, the Amazon Literary Partnership, and other generous contributions from foundations, corporations, and individuals. To these organizations and individuals we offer our heartfelt thanks.

Published by Graywolf Press
250 Third Avenue North, Suite 600
Minneapolis, Minnesota 55401

www.graywolfpress.org

Published in the United States of America

ISBN 978-1-64445-036-9 (cloth)
ISBN 978-1-64445-074-1 (paper)

2 4 6 8 9 7 5 3 1
First Graywolf Paperback, 2022

Library of Congress Control Number: 2021940560

Cover design: Jeenee Lee

Cover art: Craig Davidson

for Liz and Nick

Contents

That Was Now,
This Is Then

1

Road Trip

I could complain. I've done it before.
I could explain. I could say, for instance, that
I'm sick of being slaughtered in my life's mountain passes,
covering my own long retreat,
the rear guard of my own brutal defeat—
dysentery and frostbite and snipers,
the mules freezing to death,
blizzards whipping the famished fires until they expire,
the pathetic mosquito notes of my horn . . .
But, instead, for once, I'm keeping quiet, and maybe tomorrow
or maybe the day after or maybe the day after that
I'm just going to drive away down the coast
and not come back.
I haven't told anyone, and I won't.
I won't dim with words the radiance of my gesture.
And besides, the ones who care have guessed already.
Looking at them looking at me, I know they know
when they turn their backs I'll go.
The secrets I was planning to floor them with?
They're already packed in my trunk, in straw,
in a reinforced casket.
The bitter but herbal and medicinal truths I concocted
to revive them with?
Tomorrow or the day after or the day after that,
on the volcano beaches fringed with black sand
and heaped with tangled beds of kelp,
by the obsidian tide pools that cradle the ribbed limpet
and the rockbound star,
I'll scatter those truths to the sea breezes,
and float the secrets on the waters that the moon
reels in and plays out,

reels in and plays out,
with a little votive candle burning on their casket,
and then I'll just be there, in the sunset's coppery sheen,
in the dawn pearled by discrete, oblong, intimate clouds
that move without desire or motive.
Look at the clouds. Look how close they are.

Commas, Dashes, Ellipses, Full Stops, Question Marks

People restless on the pews downtown, people
not of the book or of the book, itchy and introspective
in the big cross-section-of-humanity room in the courthouse
on Adams Street—
apothecaries, scriveners, gendarmes, recidivists . . .
Sixty percent are happy sixty-five percent of the time.
Thirty percent are OK seventy-nine percent of the time.
One is angry—that's what the bulletins
from the ether say—and maybe will do something about it.
But not today. Today is another day.
Today is the day the self's
whispering to itself in its hundred endangered languages merges
with the sound of water running and scoring grooves in the damp,
lithic, adhesive interiors,
the limestone cavern of being
where flying mammals hang and nurse their young
and contemplate upside down the inscaped person waiting
to be called out of himself into the light of reason,
to be empaneled on a jury, here, right here in Brooklyn,
so he can judge lest he not
be judged, but forgiven, just forgiven.
Grace, with no instinct to explain itself, pouring out of every portal.
"Are you blind, that you can't see it?" "I am. I guess I am."
Communion. Submission. Detachment.
And what would I rather be doing than sitting here pretending
not to look at the rest of you, of the city and of the world,
so compelling is your exhausted, disillusioned but steadfast commitment
to the mechanisms of justice, the apparatus of democracy?
Twelve good persons and true
will be summoned from the cardinal points to . . .
but not me, I guess. The bailiff is saying,

"Go home, not you, not today."
For the hundredth time, I have been called but not chosen.
For the hundredth time, I have to shuffle into the subway station at Jay Street
where a tall, sweet-looking, willowy violinist
is playing the Chaconne with apocalyptic focus and the ghost
of a smile on her lips.
Maybe she will say yes to me.
Maybe I can stay with her always.
Maybe I can sleep on my hands at her little desk.
"I'd rather, I'd rather, I'd rather go blind than
to walk away from you, child."

Dialectic

I'm fine with hatred. Pure, precise, self-modulating.
Waxing while the world wanes.
History decrees

that we know it, and Hegel and I
both believe in history.
Hegel and I,
both of us are fine

with hatred. It will work itself out, burn itself out.
(Or maybe it won't.)

What Hegel and I can't stand
(and chime in whenever you want,
Herr Hegel)
is love.
This is what moves the sun and the stars?

Please.
"Daddy, carry me."
"I saved a piece of pie for you."
Chime in, Herr Hegel,
chime in.

Meeting (Thick)

I'll meet if you really want to meet.
I'll even meet in some small café or some
park across the way. But I won't meet for long,
and not for a minute will I look at you in your isolation,
your human isolation. Looking at yours makes me look at mine—
transparencies of each other are they, yours and mine—
and I don't have time for mine, so how could I have time for yours?
When I knew you, I had time for mine.
When I knew you, imagining my skeletal streaming
solitary oceanic swimming enlarged my dignities.
Not anymore. No time for the nostalgias, infinite, infinitesimal,
and the ones in between. No time to pretend I can sustain anyone or
even understand how they feel—to show, by the grave
downward turn of the face, the haunted eyes,
the image of an impossible inward stricken empathy.
The contradictions are unsupportable,
and I don't have time to not support mine,
so how could I not support yours, too?
I don't even have time to write this text.
See how uninflected it is, without rhetoric,
expatiation, form, concreteness, geography, weather, flora, fauna,
plain and bare (which shows you that I'm sincere)—
no Denali, no Great Rift, no seven-year trillium,
and not one phoebe in the woods getting ready to sing.

Meeting (Thin)

I'll meet if you really want to meet.
I'll even meet in some
small café or some
park across the way. But I
won't meet for long,
and not for a minute will I
look at you in your isolation,
your human isolation.
Looking at yours makes me
look at mine—
transparencies of each other are they,
yours and mine—
and I don't have time
for mine, so how could I
have time for yours?
When I knew you,
I had time for mine.
When I knew you, imagining my
skeletal streaming
solitary oceanic swimming
enlarged my dignities.
Not anymore. No time
for the nostalgias, infinite,
infinitesimal, and the ones
in between. No time to pretend
I can sustain anyone or
even understand how they feel—
to show, by the grave
downward turn of the face,
the haunted eyes,
the image of an impossible inward

stricken empathy.
The contradictions are
unsupportable,
and I don't have time to not
support mine,
so how could I not
support yours, too?
I don't even have time to write this text.
See how thin it is,
without rhetoric,
expatiation, form, concreteness,
geography, weather, flora, fauna,
plain and bare
(which shows you that I'm sincere)—
no Denali, no Great Rift,
no seven-year trillium,
and not one
phoebe in the woods getting
ready to sing.

Birding

A gray bird with a crest and a black mask.
Gilt edges the slim
tail feathers.
An eyedrop of arterial blood in a flask

of gray water is the flashing red
under the wing.
A large wader, gimlet-eyed, under
the sun's gimlet eye,

spearing frogs in the cattail
marsh. The sun itself a larger bird,
its wings manufacturing
the solar wind

that devours, that is what can devour a person—
floating in the vacuum
of perpetual space,
which is what there is and also is

itself a bird, a blackbird,
its black eye, black in black,
its sidewise look that makes you
look back.

Nemesis

Your aeroplane is pulling out its stops.
Your aeroplane is growling with its props,

pawing the tarmac with its landing gear,
streaming exhaust. That one sortie is here

that you've been fearfully anticipating.
12 o'clock high, the Red Baron is waiting

in a holding pattern behind the sun,
his mind as focused as his Gatling gun,

inviting you there, up to the skies,
you, his one absent precious prize.

He wants to silence your persiflage,
to put your picture on his fuselage.

He wants his mind relieved of you.
He wants his gun to talk to you,

embracing the murderous dialogue.
He doesn't care that you're just a dog.

Enlightenment

"It's all empty, empty,"
he said to himself.
"The sex and drugs. The violence, especially."
So he went down into the world to exercise his virtue,

thinking maybe that would help.
He taught a little kid to build a kite.
He found a cure,
and then he found a cure

for his cure.
He gave a woman at the mercy of the weather
his umbrella, even though
icy rain fell and he had pneumonia.
He settled a revolution in Spain.

Nothing worked.
The world happens, the world changes,
the world, it is written here,
in the next line,
is only its own membrane—

and, oh yes, your compassionate nature,
your compassion for our kind.

Robocall

Three or four brand-new ideas—not crisp
or sensical but, still, helpful to me—

slipped entirely from my mind
when I ran to get the phone, and heard once again
the 1-800 voice of the One saying,

"If I am He or She or They Who are here
when the last star hisses out, why am I talking to you?
I was thinking of you this morning, but why you?
Para español oprima número tres."

Another day ruined by the question of being.
When will they just let me sit under my guava tree?
—eating my guavas, thinking my quarantined thoughts,
nursing my mortified body.

Who Knows Where or When?

Now is then, now happened then,
and then again, and is going to happen again,
and then again.

The knowledge, though—
not knowledge,
exactly, but the superimposed echo,
the afterimage of

what happens again, again—changes,
or, at least, fills and backfills,
the ghost we call meaning,
the solution for which we are the problem,

which proposes
that what we know is the ghost
of what we knew again and again and again.

2

Your Living Eyes

for my mother

They wheeled you, your caregivers did, to the picture window
to watch the birds fretting at the feeder.
Then they forgot you there, and you forgot them.
A thousand years later, the Angel of Death sidled in,
disguised as a little girl,
clutching at her pinafore and chewing the ends of her pigtails.
She had a look whose vacancy was over-rehearsed,
but I hear your interview with her went well anyway.
I hear, actually, that it went better
than anybody could ever have thought it would.
She said, "Beauty and sadness are never far apart."
You said, "Bullshit."
She said, "Some birds are real, some are invisible, but which are which?"
You said, "Back off, bitch."
She stared out the window. Her eyes narrowed, but they didn't touch.
What was she seeing, what was she saying to herself?
Do I know or do I care? Enough with these impassive forces—
this one or that other one, the one
who gave you life, you who gave me life.
The yellow of the finches is as molten as ever,
splashing on the holly bushes.
The moon, pale-white inside the pale-blue morning,
dropping its panicles of glass on the bright grass,
is climbing down. But the sun is climbing up.
The world your eyes see is the world as it really is,
and you and I are going to live in it forever,
and we will hitchhike to the Painted Hills together
and hop a freight back home.

Collins Ferry Landing

for my father

Only rivers bottom out like this.
Only rivers bottom out with this kind of conviction.
Not humans, or, at least, not humans as
indisputably human as you were,
trapped in consciousness's surplus, exilic,
animalized absurdity, writhing in its contradictions—
you, the shyest person we hardly ever knew,
the solitary we hardly ever knew.
You the fatalist. Your favorite sentence
"It is what it is." (Yes, it is, it really is.)
Only the negative constructions pertain with you.
Nothing to allegorize or ring changes on
with you. Nothing occluded. Nothing with which
to make analogies or metaphors.
Never not meaning what you said, never not transparent.
Never could you have been like this river,
acquiescent to, and companionable with, Earth,
supple, reconciled, patient
while trapped between the high banks,
narrowing itself, widening itself,
sinuous through the industrial places—
slag heaps on either side, coal barges booming down its waters—
and placid and fructifying among the farms.
Never you with dynamics like this,
rushing limpid from the foothills;
soft-singing in the valleys;
oozing, opaque, mercuric through the marshland,
silvery, satiny, emollient, satisfied;
the rippling and dissimulating liquid medium—
not apparent to the flesh like you but the illusory

reflective surface into which we fall and drown.
Don't even imagine the flexibilities,
the insinuations, the dragon and the serpent
and the river beside which
you nursed that despair the three of us who loved you best
could never coax you away from.
The cold but intact rainbow trout under the ripples
are doing what? Feeding? Dreaming? No.
They are concentrating. They don't need ears
to hear your ghost, thrashing and muttering in the brush
between the river and the road—
your ghost coming back to the place you might have
thought you should have died
(all alone were you with your disappointments)
but didn't, your ghost afraid to go back to where you
shouldn't have died but did. I met him up there.
We were shivering up there together. He asked me,
"How did I get here?"
"How do I get back?"
"Where do I go now?"

—

I have a friend. (You'll be glad to know.) She and I work together. (You'll be glad to know
I still have a job.) She's an ally. She's sympathetic. She's warmhearted. She's socially con-
scious, gentle, a decent type, and from what I've observed an excellent mother, too. Not
very smart, though. A little while after your soundless departure, I was telling her about
you. I was describing what I saw as your place (yes, yes, your highly functional place) on
the spectrum of . . . what are the right words, neurocognitive homelessness? I was de-
scribing cultures of shame evolving across millennia; economies of scarcity versus econo-
mies of surplus; civilizations teetering on the edge of time, about to take the plunge
into oblivion. Deep India, I said to her. Wonders and terrors, I said to her. Deep India,
strewn with elephants and cobras. Scorched by temples, mosques, stupas, churches,
synagogues. Cratered with poverty, hunger and thirst, storms of affliction. Shot through

with sacred rivers. They flood. They shrivel out. The sun's furious particle stream immerses the pencil-thin scavengers picking sustenance from the dry riverbeds. The infant god opens his mouth to display the entire, appalling universe. I told her that long ago, when the Earth was still flat, you made your pinched, solitary, tramp-freighter journey from there to here—Colombo, Suez, across the Middle Sea, then over the far edge. I was talking privation; I was talking history; I was talking injustice. I was getting wound up and indignant. That was what must have triggered her inimitable gift for the sentimental non sequitur. She put her right hand on my left arm and said, "He'll always be with you. In your heart." See what I mean? See what I mean? Not if she had said one bright morning we'd meet up again in Heaven (and I wouldn't put it past her to say something like that, too) would she have made me angrier. I could have kicked her shin. But (wait, don't interrupt—and, no, of course I didn't kick her shin) I'd like to explain why I kept talking to her in the aftermath of her idiotic outburst, why I didn't shake the dust of my feet off at her and cut her off then and there forever. Though the time in which I'm writing this overlaps yours, you'd be amazed and embarrassed if you understood the extent to which we're allowed these days, encouraged even, to indulge feelings and succumb to motives and express resentments and make demands offensive to reason that a mind with an experience like yours, a burden of discipline, a resignation, and a silence like yours, a mind like yours cowled by melancholy, would consider disreputable, even shocking. I'm sad to say you won't be surprised that I've taken advantage of this license. I've indulged, openly and shamelessly—and, also, secretly—more times than I'm willing to remember. But I want you to understand that at this moment my talking was anything but self-indulgent. I was confused in the weeks after you died, and my confusion didn't derive from the universal fact that a parent's death is too strangely shaped for a child of theirs to grasp with any confidence but from the fact that I myself was becoming strangely shaped. I was crying (bawling at times) and grieving in the way I imagine I was expected to, in conformity with generally accepted principles of grief; but, also—don't get judgmental; I'm pretty sure I'm not alone in this—I wasn't just feeling grief but congratulating myself for it. I was seeing myself as the star of my loss, its protagonist, treading the boards, pacing under the proscenium arch of bereavement. Some part of me was saying, "Finally, reality. I've heard so much about it." That wasn't the real strangeness, though. It was this: this sin of self-awareness, this dramatization of the self, this consequentiality of consciousness, this aestheticization, this the most pathetic of all the assertions of the self as it stumbles across its blasted heath of existence was leading to a separation of self from self that was making apparent another person underneath. Another person suddenly arrived inside me. Another person, as real as the person typing this, but detached, outside the world itself and growing huge in relation to it. Another person was standing at the crossroads of time and space, shirtless, shoeless, but dressed in a nice suit, on the outside looking in, curious but indifferent to being and not being, both of which he understood as accidental and impossible. The free person, the truly free, free from time, space, the world. Don't roll your eyes, this was actually happening. Cool and supercilious before a million universes, Whitman says, or something like that. In the years when you were angry with me, and frightened for me, the search for this person haunted my mind. But now that I was he, he was the last person I wanted to be. The distance I suddenly had achieved wasn't joyous. It was unendurable. This is why I kept talking and talking, whenever I could, climbing hand over hand up the rope of words to get back to my ordinary, unenlightened life. I was clinging to other people with words. I was gripping them by their lapels. I couldn't let them go. The knowledge I had I didn't want. I knew, though, probably for the first time in my life, what I did want. I wanted the details. I wanted to be sitting on the living-room couch, watching *Jeopardy!* with you.

—

I get up in the middle of the night.
I go to the bathroom and micturate.
I come back and lie in bed wide awake.
I can't forget, I can't forget.

In the dark room, the severed wire
sparks and sparks uselessly
that once was that living wire
we shared alone,

across which, at those few piercing moments
in all our interactions,
what we call our selves
traded places. You saw yourself

through my eyes and I saw myself
through yours. These moments ping
my optic nerves alive.
Your looking at you through me

the last time you waved goodbye,
your walker holding the storm door open,
your t-shirt loose around
your shrunken chest.

My looking at me through you
the first time you waved goodbye—
sixteen months old, my hair not cut yet,
sitting in the sunlight

on the red masonry floor,
the sun entering through the open door,
the two of us on both its sides.
And then, the two of us

looking down at our four feet
on the frozen Middle American street—
on our way
to the Saturday premiere matinee

of *How the West Was Won*.
I'm matching you stride for stride.
Our four feet are moving like two feet,
and we are alive.

City of Grief

No one needs an explanation
here for what happened.
"It happened" is the explanation.
No one here belongs to a
race, an empire, a nation,
only to this unmappable,
landlocked, film-noir city
situated in eternity.
They live by night here.
The time here is local time.
The crime is local crime.
The girl with the name
she stole from her dead sister,
the dead man in the lake
know that things are
forever the same.
Sameness is their essence.
Nothing here is sinister
because nothing is at stake.
Everything is null and void
of depth, of resonance,
not real but celluloid.
Yesterday was yesterday,
today is today, and
no one cares why
one becomes the other—
no one but the private eye
that is, the gumshoe, the
bird dog standing in for us,
our body double, our fedora-
sporting, anachronistic,

obsolete consciousness,
who is always tortured by
what he can't understand,
who hires himself
to investigate himself,
who cooks his dinner for one
and tries to think through
what can't be thought through.
The black wine is aerating.
The pasta is limp and waiting
to be sauced and tossed.
There is a clue to find.
There is an innocence
to establish and an anguish in
him he needs to destroy
before it destroys him, an
anguish so pure it almost
feels like joy.

Cliffhanging

for Tom Lux

The forces out to kill us with their benevolence
are more crazed now than they were when you were alive.
And more focused, too. Our ingratitude excites them.
They're bubbling with remedies.
Their providential impulses are a nimbus of knives.
Their need to tell us they love us, love us,
with all their love in vain . . .

You said before you died that this would happen.
Thanks for the warning. You didn't let me know, though,
that even our phantom selves would come after us,
crawling out of the poems we made.
They don't care about the transparent skin we wrapped them in
so they could watch their organs pulsing within.
All they know is that we made their eyes too bright.
They see more than they can stand,
more than we ever could or would. They see the unending savagery
that we could never really bear to see,
and so we consigned our sight to them.
They hate us for it. They've cut the phone lines,
and are chain-sawing the front door.

I'm a little worried about myself because
all this hostility from every quarter bothers me
much less than it should. Why the disconnect? I can't figure it out.
And it's long past time to take precautions.
The great wave that breaks through the crust of the world
is rising and rising and lifting me far inland,
only to suck me back and drop me dangling by one arm
on the edge of the half-eaten cliff.

I won't let myself fall, but I don't want to pull myself up.
I'm ambivalent. I'm ambivalent forever now.
But if you were here, looking down on me and saying,
"Grab my hand, grab my hand," I would, I know, I surely would.

Goya's Mired Men Fighting with Cudgels

The violence done to the mind by the weaponized
word or image is bad.
We can live with it, though.
We can understand it. Or we can try. And we
can consider ourselves lucky, which we are.
Nothing can be understood
about the blunt-force trauma to the head.
The percussion grenade.
The helmet-to-helmet hit at an aggregate speed
of forty miles an hour.
No concussion protocol comprehends the self's
delicate apparatus crumpled in the wide pan of the brain.
The roof collapsing in Aleppo.
The beam slamming the frontal lobe.
The drone, the terror by night and day.
He wanted to remember it all,
to fix the image cradled inside the image
of itself, itself, itself
down the facing mirrors of future and past,
and then he wanted to be left to die there,
in the ditch where he was cudgeled
down and under—
groundwater seeping into his mouth,
himself becoming ground water.
But he felt a hand reach down and grab him
by the collar and yank him back up
and set him on his feet.
And as he steadied himself, he thought,
This compassion he feels for me as his
mirror enemy, image, brother in wrath,
and that I feel for him,

this compassion is the compassion that those
who see themselves in agony feel.
But there is the other compassion, the one
felt by those who see agony in themselves,
which the deaf master will feel
when he imagines us poised and ready to recapitulate
our thinking's frozen violence—
the great deaf master,
living in the villa of the deaf,
where he will paint us in silent pastels.

Night City

What happened to the city that made us
promises, promises we had the luxury
to believe or not?
Night caved its streets,

collapsed its buildings,
and crushed its ten million screens.
And, now, from the crushed screens
the flat,

translucent images
extrude themselves, escape, and flow, flat,
over the rubble . . .

flat images desperate to become round,
flailing across the river from one dimension
to the next—

brutalized children, drowned fathers, drowning
in the river and then in
the eye and then in the mind—

flat images stealing quietly
over the rubble,
flowing under the cracked sills and over

the broken stairs
and into the city's caved beds
to wrap around the sleepers like
cellophane,

wrapping the complicated sleepers in
simple suffering, the sleepers
huddling in their dreams,

muffled by their longings, their ears
muffled, while mobs with torches
rage on the rubble.

3

The Idol of the Tribe

I look at you with my vexed eye.
I look at you with my hostile eye.
I look at you with my hostile and vexed eye.
My hostile, vexed eye is a wrench.

My vexed eye is a socket wrench.
My vexed and hostile socket-wrench eye twists
the bolt that hinges your mandible free
from its frozen grooves.

You scream, but we go on turning,
I and my eye.
I know what I'm into.
I know what I've been put here for.

I've been put here for you.
The ducks in the marshland line up
by the mallows they resemble, but
no miracle of nature can delay me.

Snow, rain, heat, etc.
can't stay me from the completion
of my dismantling you, my
being rid of you.

I remove your jaw. I lay it aside.
Your neck bone I disconnect
from your shoulder bone,
your shoulder bone I disconnect

from your breast bone,
your breast bone from your back bone,
your back bone from each rib,
each rib from the sound of your lord.

Your tinted waters laden with debris
stream from your split flanks.
Your truths take on their true proportions.
How small they always were—

not false, but trivial.
I make a heap out of you.
You're not dead, of course.
You said yourself you can never die,

so that was never the point.
The point is this: here, around me,
you're disassembled, you're a junkyard,
you've been sacrificed.

Man and Woman Talking

Lighted room. Man and Woman enter talking.

—I mean, we built the world.

—What do you mean?

—You know what I mean.
   Calling him masculine.
   Calling him masculine, as if masculine
   explains why you don't like him,
   as if masculine explains the hostility . . .
   something is required, something more than that
   is required, OK?

—I don't know what you mean.

—What I mean is that we,
   and that means men, we men,
   built the world,
   so calling him masculine as if,
   you know what I mean,
   as if that's kaput, that's all you need to say to . . .
   to justify the hostility, is . . .

—What do you mean, men built the world?

—Airplanes.
   Air-conditioning.
   Amoxicillin.
   Chartres.
   Transcendentalism.
   Calculus.
   Obviously.
   Plato.

—Right. So now he's Plato because he's a guy.
   You should hear yourself sometime:
   "Men built the world."
   Nyah. Nyah. Nyah.

—I hear myself fine.
   I hear myself beautifully.
   So then you tell me why exactly don't you like him?
   I mean, you've known him forever.
   You introduced us.

—What do you want me to say?
   I don't like him because he reminds me of you?
   What do you want me to say?
   What do you want me to say?

Blackout.

Lights come back up. Woman enters in a bathrobe talking to herself.

Oh God what a pill
The constant subsurface ruptures of self-glorifying need
The need venting its fumes
The need under a mental landscape stinking with theories
The mental landscape every inch ploughed under built over
The need under the brain fissures venting leaking
The suppurating sores of his inner landscape
The gaping fissures oozing magmatic pus
The sulfurous sighs
They say we leak
They say we keep showing them our insides
The crammed insides they don't want to see
The slick organs they have them too
That is disgusting projection
I can't let him bait me like that though

What is the matter with me
Why can't I be like Dominique
Blow it off blow it off
Walking around without a clue
Performing themselves without a clue
We're all performers he'll say life is performance
Another goddam theory
No we're not
We're not we're better than that we have to be
This isn't playacting this isn't a movie
We built the world yeah right
Transcendentalism yeah right
Infect the blankets with smallpox
Sell them to the Indians so they die die die
Then put up your skyscraper mausoleums
Your missile silos
Oh God oh God
Oh God

Blackout.

Lights come back up. Enter Man stage left, reading out loud from a book.
He walks across the stage while reading and exits stage right.

"I saw Eternity the other night,
Like a great ring of pure and endless light,
All calm, as it was bright;
And round beneath it, Time in hours, days, years,
Driv'n by the spheres
Like a vast shadow mov'd; in which the world
And all her train were hurl'd. . . ."

Blackout.

Marriage

You keep complaining that there are two people inside me—

the one confident, decisive, ironic;
the other a raging cripple
who never took to the nipple,
whose life has been one long
episode of colic.

Just admit you don't know which one you like better,
which one rings your bell.

I happen to like them both.
I make the one drive the other around and around
the glistening night streets of our town
to try and calm him,
calm him down.

I want them to be inseparable, inevitable.
I don't want the children to suffer.

Visiting San Francisco

I wanted to curl up
in the comfortable cosmic melancholy of my past,
in the sadness of my past being passed.
I wanted to tour the museum of my antiquities
and look at the sarcophagi there.
I wanted to wallow like a water buffalo in the cool,
sagacious mud of my past,
so I wrote you and said I'd be in town and could we meet.
But you think my past is your present.
You wouldn't relent, you wouldn't agree
to dinner or a cup of coffee or even a bag of peanuts
on a bench in North Beach.
You didn't want to curl up or tour or wallow with me.
You're still mad, long after the days
have turned into decades, about the ways I let you down.
The four hundred thousand ways.
Maybe I would be, too.
But people have done worse to me.
I don't think I'm being grotesque when I tell you
I've been flayed and slayed and force-fed anguish.
I've been a human cataract
plunging through a noose and going to pieces on the rocks.
I've been a seagull tethered to Alcatraz.
What can I say, what more can I say, how much more
vulnerable can I be, to persuade you
now that I've persuaded myself?
Why can't you just let it go?
Well, at least I'm in San Francisco.
San Francisco, where the homeless are most at home—
crouching over their tucker bags under your pollarded trees—
because your beauty is as free to them

as to the domiciled in their
dead-bolt domiciles, your beauty is as free to
the innocent as to the guilty.
The fog has burned off.
In a cheap and windy room on Russian Hill
a man on the run unwraps the bandages
swaddling his new face, his reconstructed face,
and looks in the mirror and sees
the face of Humphrey Bogart. Only here
could such a thing happen.
It was really always you, San Francisco,
time won't ever darken my love for you,
San Francisco.

Who Is This Guy?

Now that I'm dead, too, just like the living dead on TV,
fat chance that the merely living will be saved
by doing what they did when I was merely living—
nailing their doors shut against me,
hurricane-proofing the windows,
positioning snipers at the embrasures.
Now that I have a dead army, too, fat chance
for the living, for the strength of my dead legions
is the eternal and irrepressible
strength of nonbeing, nonbeing that terrified
being into birthing the world,
and then licked the afterbirth clean
until the world gleamed with nothingness.
Fat chance for the living in the face of that.
Quail they will in the sensible storm of nonbeing,
and weep will they in the face
of my dead army's weapons: not guns and sharp swords
but the residual fragrances of their lives on earth,
the leftover aromatics of the dead, time bombs,
memory's mines in memory's fields,
each memory wrapped in a fragrance,
each memory a drop of time
around which a translucent agate has formed
redolent with what was left behind
when its owners vanished.
A molecule of honeysuckle and it is that summer night.
The long shadows. The risen full moon
casts a veil of leaf shadows over a face. The eyes swim up at you.
Then an odor of roses, but powdery and particulate.
A stewardess at the dawn of the age of universal jet travel.
Your mother holds your hand in hers.

You will be given biscuits in foil and chocolates
made in a country called Switzerland.
Then the burning maple leaves. Then the faint odor
of tin before the monsoon sweeps in.
Then the torrents in the gutter and the smashed mango pods.
Then the rainbow.
Then the rich, delicious mildew of the trailer on the floodplain.
You forgot yourself there.
You never afterwards remembered what you forgot,
never recollected yourself. You will recollect yourself now,
in these fragrances, the indices of memory and the engines
of my dead army. Now will the living know
what they were meant to mean, and they
will know that what they've lost
isn't lost at all, but is there, right there,
dancing on the other side of time—
what they were and what it was,
what it meant and what it means
just on the other side of time.
The confusion can't be endured.
The longing is as if it were a knife, and for that longing alone—
piercing and inevitable—
the living, the beautiful living, would, if I weren't already dead,
kill me again and again.

North American Sequence

Not liberation, exactly, but at least a relief to know
that after another long, exasperating
journey into the self—
the meadows choked with pigweed,
the coppices deranged, the spinneys disheveled,
the fosses slimed and slippery,
the Chevy Impalas, their tires stripped,
rusting on concrete blocks in the front yards,
the roads sunk under mud,
the hills on fire, the crocodile deltas—
you can emerge and re-enter the public sphere
and make yourself presentable again
as someone other people can look at and look past
in the sphere they inhabit,
the globe of reason and sphere of discourse
pure and simple, where to observe and anatomize
its latest structural transformation
into an even more unthinkable strangeness
is a species of fun, and, also, a part
of the strangeness. And what a relief that no one
in the public sphere cares,
really, who or what you are;
they're all busy making gossip out of experience;
they're all indifferent to traumas, yours or theirs;
they're all fed up with the inner life;
and, besides, the thinkers of the public sphere
now say there is no inner life.
The inner life was a big misunderstanding,
with unfortunate historical consequences.
There are, though, some fine buildings here,
oblong, square, round, tall, short—

the tall ones very tall, the short ones short enough—
and the inhabitants, also, are
tall and short, square and round,
white and black and brown, denizens,
loving their geometries, their symmetries,
while their destinies diversify
in the dry, lightly scented air.
How anybody could love destinies like theirs
is something you don't
have to worry about. What is asked of you only
is that you listen to their voices—
their orisons, vows, shouts of joy,
their raging, hateful imprecations,
their love chats and griefs—
joining with other voices to form a stream
of voices, among other streams
that will unite in rivers blue as the sky is blue,
and flow to the cobalt ocean,
there to swell its waters until
the pressure of the swelling becomes so great
the waters particulate, evaporate
again, and rise, lighter than air, rise and rise
to come athwart the cold of space,
the killing cold, the touch of which crystallizes
their essences so that they fall as snow
and bury in concave blowing drifts another lost
neighborhood of the public sphere,
abandoned now to the blizzard and to you,
the solitary walker standing in an
itinerant pool of light below the single streetlamp
in the neighborhood where once,
fifty years apart, were born
Al Capone, Chicago gangster,
and Jennie Jerome, Winston Churchill's mother.

Thunderstruck

The house collapsed and I was crushed under the rubble,
pulverized, but here I am,
walking around as if I were alive—

the swain,
with an oxeye daisy in my buttonhole,
the bitter voluptuary, never satisfied,
the three-legged dog,
the giant under the tiny parasol at
the Fontaine-de-Vaucluse,
the only Abyssinian in the choir of the
Abyssinian Baptist Church.

(Somebody must have done a self-portrait of me.)

Just amazing. I think I could wrap my arms all the way around
the 24,901-miles-circumferenced Earth.

The Estuary

The brown bear living near the estuary,
and wading out when the tide swells and the salmon run,
during the days of the dwindling salmon runs,
and slapping with his big right paw a hook-nosed fish
whipsawing inland to spawn,
the ambidextrous bear,
furred like the forest from which he emerged,
waddling into the unteachable waters
to swat the salmon out the fast-running tide
and catch the red salmon in his mouth
and toss and juggle the sockeye salmon
thrashing and drowning in the air—
and when he's expressed himself completely
he catches with his jaw the self
that swam ten thousand miles to the estuary
and daintily, mincingly, with one paw grasping
the caudal fin and the other the head,
eats that salmon as if he were we
and the fish an ear of boiled corn—
that bear is a bear about whom rich and complicated
feelings can be felt. That is a bear from whom ideas
about the state of nature can be derived.
Cruelty is the wrong word to describe
the pleasure he gets from playing with his lunch.
Play and life are the same thing to him,
art and life, life and death.
Creation impinging on a consciousness
clear and crystalline. Pinpoint revelatory
explosions unsoiled by words, unbesmirched.
Creation clambering out of the waters,
shaking itself off, creation

surrounding itself with itself . . .

Stay down on the pavement where you just fell in a heap
like a bag of laundry, just stay there. Move even a
little and you might damage something else.
You've already done plenty of damage.
Stay down, supine. Stay down,
and let the giant buildings loom over you, let them
in their abstract imperium stun you with their indifference.
Wasn't that the reason you built them in the first place?
Stay down, stay down, and ask yourself:
"Could I be the bear in this fable?"
"Could I be the fish?"
"Could I be whoever is imagining all this?"

Soliloquy

All the experts say I'm sane.
Some even say I might acquire insight someday.
Some even introduce me to their kids.
What could be more reassuring than that?
Also, when it comes to my body, I like it,
and I care for it. I read the latest research.
My diet is 80/20 alkalinity to acidity.
My body is a temple wherein my spirit—
in which I also believe,
like any other normal person—
is sublimely housed. So why on a train platform
just before the engine barrels in
do I feel a thrill rising from my groin to my solar plexus
and imagine jumping?
Why on a puddle-hopper from one midsize,
midwestern city to another,
going from one sales meeting to another
(and I not only like myself I like
my job; our market share is growing;
business class is great, the leg room
and the free drinks),
do I watch myself unbuckling my seat belt,
creeping down the aisle,
wrenching counter-clockwise the emergency exit's cold,
recalcitrant shank, kicking open the door to
the beautiful and spacious skies,
and plunging five miles down
past the goshawks rising on their thermals,
plunging to America and its billowing farms
with fields dotted here and there
with big lozenges of hay wrapped in white plastic

moist with the morning dew?
Every time, every time—the exquisite acceleration
down the steeples of the air 32 feet
per second per second,
the overheated mind ventilating at last,
the ground coming up very fast . . . though not
to hit the ground, no, no
(what a piece of work that would turn out to be),
or to be slammed like a caddis fly against the train's
bullet head, traumatizing the poor, pitiable engineer—
a guy just like me, doing his job,
and suddenly he finds himself
face to face with horror? . . .
no, not that, not that, never that, but, simply,
for the moment before the last—
the penultimate moment
and the moment inside the penultimate moment,
and the moment inside that and that and that . . .
I have heard it said, I have heard it is written,
I have read of it, and I have understood
by reason's light within me,
that the moment I am speaking of
stretches across eternity,
and never moves on to become the next moment,
and to be suspended inside it is to see
our pinpoint presence among the stars reversed,
and the stars themselves coalescing
into a perfect orb small enough to hold
in the palm of the hand, from the center of which
being shall look into your eyes.
Who wouldn't jump for a chance at that? Yesterday,
in the General Mitchell International Airport—
in the city of Milwaukee, in the state of Wisconsin—
I was served an arresting fortune cookie

at the Chinese restaurant there.
It read, "Life cries out *Be*."
O ancient sages of the Middle Kingdom,
of course, of course . . .

To the Reader

I'm writing this so I can tell you that what you're thinking
about me is exactly what I'm thinking
about you.

What you're reading is exactly what you're writing,
by the light of a taper, deep inside yourself,
at your walnut secretary.

These words are saying
what those words say, and these and those

are those and these, mine and yours, and have no meaning,
only form. Talk about

being one with others!
We correspond 1 to 1, and there is a grandeur in this.
You'll understand that someday.

Just now, though, you're stupefied at this
spooky action at a distance.

So would I be, and I am.

Acknowledgments

Grateful acknowledgment is made to the following publications and sites, in which versions of these poems first appeared: *The American Poetry Review* ("Collins Ferry Landing"); *BOMB* ("Soliloquy"); *Literary Imagination* ("Who Knows Where or When?," "City of Grief"); *The National* ("To the Reader"); *The New Republic* ("Marriage"); *The New Yorker* ("Cliffhanging," "Visiting San Francisco," "The Estuary"); *Ocean State Review* ("Robocall"); *Peripheries* ("North American Sequence"); *Poetry* ("Thunderstruck"); *Poets.org* ("Road Trip," "Enlightenment," "Goya's Mired Men Fighting with Cudgels"); *Salmagundi* ("Commas, Dashes, Ellipses, Full Stops, Question Marks," "Your Living Eyes"); *Virginia Quarterly Review* ("Man and Woman Talking," "The Idol of the Tribe," "Who Is This Guy?," "Night City"); *The Yale Review* ("Meeting," "Birding").

The author would also like to thank the Corporation of Yaddo and New England College's Elizabeth Yates McGreal Writer-in-Residence program, which provided time and resources crucial to the completion of this book.

Vijay Seshadri was born in Bangalore, India, and came to America as a small child. He is the author of four other collections of poems: *3 Sections*, winner of the Pulitzer Prize; *The Long Meadow*, winner of the James Laughlin Award of the Academy of American Poets; *Wild Kingdom*; and *The Disappearances* (HarperCollins India), and many essays, reviews, and memoir fragments. He currently teaches at Sarah Lawrence College and lives in Brooklyn, New York.

The text of *That Was Now, This Is Then* is set in Arno Pro.
Book design by Rachel Holscher. Composition by Bookmobile Design
and Digital Publisher Services, Minneapolis, Minnesota.
Manufactured by Versa Press on acid-free, 30 percent postconsumer wastepaper.